Ground Governance

A Practical Guide to Implementing Data Governance That Works

By
Dr. Adetokunbo Ajibola

MAPLE
PUBLISHERS

Grounded Governance A Practical Guide to Implementing Data Governance That Works

Author: Dr. Adetokunbo Ajibola

Copyright © 2025 Dr. Adetokunbo Ajibola

The right of Dr. Adetokunbo Ajibola to be identified as author of this work has been asserted by the author in accordance with section 77 and 78 of the Copyright, Designs and Patents Act 1988.

ISBN 978-1-83538-724-5 (Paperback)
      978-1-83538-725-2 (Hardback)
      978-1-83538-726-9 (E-Book)

Book Cover, Illustrations and Layout by:

White Magic Studios

www.whitemagicstudios.co.uk

Published by:

Maple Publishers

Fairbourne Drive, Atterbury,

Milton Keynes,

MK10 9RG, UK

www.maplepublishers.com

ABOUT THE AUTHOR

Dr. Adetokunbo Ajibola is a seasoned multi award winning internationally recognised data & analytics leader, Chief Data Officer, and strategic advisor with over 25 years of experience delivering enterprise-wide data governance and transformation across financial services, utilities, pharmaceuticals, telecommunications, and government sectors — including high-impact programmes in the Middle East.

Known in the industry as *The Data Evangelist*, Adetokunbo has championed data as a business asset long before it became a boardroom buzzword. He has served as a trusted leader and consultant to multinational corporations, regulators, and public sectors, architecting governance frameworks that are not only compliant — but business-enabling.

He is the Founder and CEO of Berkeley Data Strategists, where he has personally trained and mentored over 4,000 professionals into successful data careers. His work spans data quality, master data management, metadata, AI governance, and AI change — always grounded in practical execution.

Adetokunbo holds engineering degrees from the University of Sheffield, a Doctor of Philosophy (Honoris Causa) in Business Administration, and certifications including CDMP, DCAM, and MDQM. He is a frequent keynote speaker at global summits and a respected voice in shaping the future of data leadership.

DEDICATION

To my beloved wife, Eseosa-

Your unwavering love, grace, and wisdom have carried me through every season.

You have been my calm in the chaos, my strength in uncertainty, and my constant reminder of what truly matters.

This book exists because of your belief in me — even when the journey was long, and the nights were late.

Thank you for your patience, your prayers, and your partnership. You are the heartbeat of everything I build.

To my amazing children, Ayomide and Olasubomi —

You inspire me daily to lead with integrity and purpose.

May this book remind you that excellence is possible, dreams are worth pursuing, and your name carries power.

My greatest legacy will always be the example I set for you.

With all my love — this is for you.

APPRECIATION

This book is the result of not just personal experience, but a shared journey — one shaped by the trust, support, and collaboration of so many remarkable people.

To my clients around the world — thank you for allowing me into your boardrooms, your data challenges, and your bold transformations. Your trust gave me the platform to turn theory into practice and vision into value.

To my friends, who encouraged this book long before the first word was written — your belief in me kept this project alive, especially on the hardest days.

To my incredible mentees — over 5,000 strong — you are the heartbeat of this mission. Watching you grow into data professionals and leaders has been one of the greatest privileges of my life. You remind me daily that impact scales through people.

To the dedicated staff of Berkeley Data Strategists, thank you for embodying excellence, resilience, and purpose. Your passion powers the movement.

A special and deeply personal appreciation goes to James Essien, my Chief Operating Officer and Chief of Staff and Ayodeji Omotade, my Head of Talent Development. James and Ayodeji, your steadfastness, loyalty, and unshakable commitment have been the anchor of this vision. Your ability to lead with calm under pressure and hold the line with integrity has not only shaped this book but strengthened everything we've built.

This book is not just mine. It is ours — a testament to collective belief, collaboration, and the power of people who care.

Let us continue building a world where data is governed with purpose — and people lead with vision.

INTRODUCTION: WHY DATA GOVERNANCE FAILS — AND HOW TO MAKE IT WORK

Data is everywhere. It fuels decisions, drives innovation, and powers everything from customer experiences to regulatory compliance. And yet, despite billions spent on systems, software, and strategy, many still struggle with a basic truth: **they don't trust their data**.

The root cause? Governance failure.

Too often, data governance is misunderstood. It's treated as a compliance exercise, a box to check, or worse — an IT problem. The result is predictable: resistance, confusion, shelf-ware policies, and failed initiatives that never leave the strategy deck.

This book exists to change that.

Grounded Governance is built on one core belief: **data governance must be practical, people-driven, and anchored in real business value**. It should not be a theoretical framework known only to specialists, but a shared language that empowers teams, improves decisions, and safeguards trust.

Over the past 25 years, I've worked across finance, telecoms, healthcare, government, and utilities — from the boardroom to the back office — helping organisations turn governance from red tape into competitive edge. I've seen what works, what fails, and most importantly, what's missing in most governance playbooks.

This guide is different.

It bridges the **why** with the **how**. You'll learn how to:

- Build the business case for governance that gets leadership buy-in
- Design a flexible, scalable governance framework
- Define and activate roles like Data Owners and Stewards
- Write policies people actually follow
- Embed data quality, metadata, and MDM into your organisation
- Measure success with KPIs that matter
- Govern for emerging challenges — like AI ethics and regulatory risk

Whether you're a Chief Data Officer launching your first programme, a data steward struggling with ambiguity, or a business leader tired of fighting bad data, this book will give you **the roadmap to make governance work** — not just in theory, but in practice.

It's time to stop asking, 'Why don't people care about data governance?'

It's time to show them why they should — and how it can help them win.

Let's get started.

Contents

Chapter 1

Understanding Data Governance: Beyond The Buzzword

"You cannot govern what you do not understand."

Data governance has earned a reputation for being nebulous and bureaucratic — often evoked in strategy documents but rarely implemented in a way that adds business value. But at its core, data governance is not about creating red tape. It is about building trust.

What is Data Governance, Really?

At its simplest, data governance is the practice of managing data so that it is accurate, secure, accessible, and usable — not just for IT, but for the whole organisation. It is the system of decision rights, processes, and policies that ensures data is treated as a valuable corporate asset.

Why It Matters Now More Than Ever

In today's digital economy, data is the fuel for decision-making, AI, regulatory compliance, and customer trust. But without governance, data becomes a liability — fragmented, unreliable, and risky.

Real-world headlines show us why it matters:

- A global bank fined millions for inaccurate regulatory reports.
- A health tech firm breaching GDPR due to poor data handling.
- A retail giant unable to launch personalisation due to messy customer data.

These are governance failures.

Data Governance vs. Data Management

It is important to distinguish data governance from data management. Governance defines the "rules of the road". Management is about driving the car.

Governance asks: Who owns this data? Who decides how it is used? What are the acceptable quality standards? Management then executes those decisions through tools and operations.

Common Misconceptions

- *"It is an IT problem."* False. Governance is cross-functional.
- *"We just need a tool."* No. Tools enable, but frameworks lead.
- *"It slows us down."* The opposite is true when done well.

The Core Pillars

We will expand on these in the coming chapters, but every successful data governance programme is built on:

1. Clear ownership and accountability
2. Policies and standards everyone understands
3. Processes embedded into daily operations
4. Technology to scale and automate
5. Measurement and continuous improvement

This book is about showing you how to move from idea to implementation — from theory to action. Whether you're starting from scratch or rebooting a failed initiative, the next chapters will give you everything you need to establish and grow data governance in your organisation.

UP NEXT

Chapter 2 – "Data governance is a team sport — and you need the whole bench to win."

Launching a data governance initiative without preparing the ground is like pouring concrete without a mould — it will harden, but not in a usable shape. This chapter covers how to assess your organisation's readiness, identify key players, and begin securing the buy-in that will sustain your programme.

Chapter 2

Laying The Groundwork: Assessing Readiness And Getting Buy-In

1. Know Where You're Starting From

Before you do anything, you need to answer: *How mature is our current data environment?*

Conducting a Data Governance Maturity Assessment helps determine:

- If **leadership** understands the value of data governance
- If business units currently "own" their data
- If data quality issues are being tracked or resolved
- Whether roles like Data Owners or Stewards exist (even informally)
- If current tools (Excel, SharePoint, ERPs) support or hinder governance

Use one of these recognised models:

- DAMA-DMBOK maturity model
- Gartner's 5-Level Maturity Scale
- DCAM (Data Management Capability Assessment Model)

Even a simple RAG (Red-Amber-Green) assessment across key areas (ownership, quality, metadata, tooling, etc.) can highlight gaps and quick wins.

2. Identify and Map Your Stakeholders

You will need to build a coalition of support across business, IT, risk, and compliance. Start by identifying who has a stake in the success of data governance:

- Executive Sponsors (CIO, CDO, CFO): Their support unlocks funding and visibility.

- Data Owners (e.g. heads of Finance, Marketing): They are accountable for data domains.
- Data Stewards: Operational staff who know the data and manage it daily.
- IT/Architecture Teams: Enable technical tooling and enforce standards.
- Regulatory/Compliance: Keep governance aligned with GDPR, HIPAA, SOX, etc.

Tip: Run stakeholder interviews or surveys to understand their pain points. Ask:
- What data issues are most painful in your team?
- What would success in data governance look like to you?
- What concerns do you have about a formal governance process?

This builds empathy and helps you position governance as a solution, not a burden.

3. Secure Executive Sponsorship Early

Without visible and vocal support from the top, governance efforts stall. Executives need to:
- Commit resources (people, budget, time)
- Back governance mandates publicly
- Resolve conflicts when silos resist change

Create a 1-pager Business Case that includes:
- A clear definition of data governance
- 3–5 pain points or risk events (e.g. regulatory breaches, reporting delays)
- Cost of inaction (e.g. lost productivity, reputational damage)
- Benefits of action (e.g. improved analytics, trust, compliance)
- A proposed roadmap for the first 6–12 months

Make it tangible. Speak the language of risk, revenue, and reputation.

4. Define the Vision and Scope

Don't start too big. Begin with a "lighthouse" scope — a focused domain (e.g., customer data, financial reporting, product catalogue) that:
- Has clear data challenges

- Crosses multiple teams (to prove governance's value)
- Ties directly to a strategic initiative

Craft a Vision Statement like:

"To ensure that our customer data is accurate, trusted, and accessible to support regulatory reporting, better customer experience, and advanced analytics." Limit scope early. You can scale later.

5. Communicate Early and Often

Governance fails in silence. People need to know:

- What is changing — and why
- Who is involved — and what it means for them
- How it improves their day-to-day work

Start simple.

- Hold a "Data Governance Town Hall".
- Share pain points, plans, and invite feedback.
- Use internal newsletters, intranet pages, and pilot teams to spread the message.

Tip: Frame governance as enablement, not enforcement.

6. Checklist: Laying the Groundwork

- ✓ Conducted a baseline maturity assessment
- ✓ Identified and interviewed stakeholders
- ✓ Built a business case with pain points and benefits
- ✓ Secured executive sponsorship
- ✓ Defined a clear vision and scoped the first use case
- ✓ Started internal communications

UP NEXT

Chapter 3 – Building the Business Case: Aligning with Strategic Objectives

In the next chapter, we will dig deeper into how to make the case for data governance compelling to decision-makers — with ROI models, compliance drivers, and real-world examples from finance, healthcare, and telecom.

Chapter 3

Building The Business Case: Aligning With Strategic Objectives

"Data governance doesn't sell itself — it must speak the language of business."

While many organisations know they need data governance, few take the time to clearly articulate *why now, and why it matters*. A strong business case connects governance to what your organisation already cares about: compliance, customer satisfaction, growth, and operational efficiency.

This chapter will walk you through how to frame data governance as a strategic enabler — not a side project — using real-world pain points, financial logic, and cross-functional alignment.

1. Start With Pain — Not Principles

Most executives won't rally around "data stewardship". But they will rally around avoiding a fine, accelerating time to market, or fixing broken customer experiences.

Identify 3–5 business pain points. Examples include:

- Inaccurate reporting leading to regulatory scrutiny
- Revenue loss due to incorrect customer or product data
- Delays in product launches caused by data quality issues
- Duplicate records in CRM causing marketing waste
- Time wasted in reconciling inconsistent reports

Pair each with a real example — something your stakeholders have felt. E.g.:

"Last quarter, our monthly regulatory report had to be refiled due to an address

formatting issue in our core banking system. This delayed compliance, cost us £10,000 in penalties, and required 3 Full Time Employees (FTEs) to manually fix the issue."

2. Link Governance to Strategic Goals

Next, connect data governance to the organisation's top priorities. These often include:

- **Digital transformation:** Governance enables clean, integrated data for automation, AI, and cloud migration.
- **Regulatory compliance:** Governance ensures traceability and defensible controls.
- **Customer experience:** Accurate, accessible data improves personalisation, service, and retention.
- **Operational efficiency:** Reduces duplication, manual work, and firefighting.
- **Revenue growth:** Reliable insights drive smarter decision-making and targeting.

Create a matrix like this:

Strategic Priority	Data Governance Contribution
Regulatory Compliance	Data lineage, ownership, and audit trails
Digital Transformation	Unified standards, metadata, and trusted inputs
Customer Centricity	Clean master data and consistent customer identifiers
Operational Efficiency	Defined ownership and fewer data disputes
Growth Through Analytics	Higher confidence in reporting and predictions

This positions data governance as an enabler, not an overhead.

3. Quantify the Cost of Inaction

Nothing motivates a business-like risk. Highlight what the organisation stands to lose if governance is delayed:

- Penalties and legal exposure (GDPR, NDPR, HIPAA, CCPA)

- Cost of poor-quality data (often estimated at 15–25% of revenue)
- Loss of trust and reputation due to inaccurate reporting or service failures
- Missed business opportunities because of untrusted analytics

Use internal data if possible. If not, cite industry stats:

IBM estimates that poor data quality costs U.S. businesses over $3.1 trillion annually.

Gartner reports that organisations lose an average of $12.9 million/year due to bad data.

4. Forecast the ROI of Governance

Though governance does not generate revenue directly, it enables benefits that can be modelled. Here is how:

Benefit	Example Estimate
Time saved on manual corrections	3 FTEs x $70K = $210K/year
Reduced regulatory risk	Avoiding £50K fine/year + £100K remediation cost
Improved campaign ROI	10% lift via cleaner customer data = $300K uplift
Faster reporting cycle	25% reduction in effort = $150K in efficiency gains

Use conservative assumptions. Your goal is credibility, not hype.

5. Include a Phased Roadmap and Budget

Decision-makers want to know what they are signing up for. Include a simple plan:

Phase 1 (0–3 months): Discovery & Mobilisation

- Maturity assessment
- Governance framework design
- Data ownership model

Phase 2 (4–6 months): Pilot Use Case (e.g., Customer Data)

- Implement data standards
- Establish stewardship roles
- Deploy metadata tool (optional)

Phase 3 (7–12 months): Scale and Sustain

- Governance council formalised
- KPI dashboard for data quality
- Expand to finance and operations

Include high-level budget estimates:

- Tool licences (if applicable)
- Training and communications
- Dedicated headcount (full-time or fractional)

6. Pre-Empt Objections

Be ready for pushback. Common concerns:

- "We do not have the time." → "That is exactly why we need governance — to reduce rework."
- "We cannot afford this right now." → "We are already paying the cost of bad data — we are just not tracking it."
- "We tried this before, and it failed." → "We are starting small with clear accountability and measurable outcomes."

Checklist: Building Your Business Case

- ✓ Identified key business pain points
- ✓ Aligned with strategic objectives
- ✓ Quantified cost of inaction and ROI
- ✓ Developed a phased implementation plan
- ✓ Prepared for objections and resistance

Up Next

Chapter 4 – Designing Your Data Governance Framework

Now that your stakeholders are aligned and energised, it is time to structure your governance initiative. In Chapter 4, we will cover frameworks, operating models, and how to define what good looks like — from the ground up.

Chapter 4

Designing Your Data Governance Framework

"A framework turns ambition into structure — and structure into action."

With buy-in secured and your business case approved, it is time to design your governance framework — the blueprint that defines how data will be governed across your organisation. This chapter walks through the key components of a scalable, flexible framework that works in practice, not just on paper.

1. What Is a Data Governance Framework?

A data governance framework is the operating model for how decisions about data are made, enforced, and evolved. It answers the "who, what, when, and how" of data ownership, policy creation, standard enforcement, and issue resolution.

It typically includes:

- Guiding principles and objectives
- Organisational structure and roles
- Policies and standards
- Processes for issue management and change control
- Tooling and technology enablement
- Metrics and monitoring mechanisms

2. Choose a Model that Fits Your Organisation

There is no "one-size-fits-all" model. The right approach depends on your size, industry, data maturity, and regulatory landscape. But most frameworks fall into one of three categories:

Model Type	Description	Best For
Centralised	One team or CDO office owns and governs data	Small to mid-sized orgs; strong central IT
Federated	Shared ownership between business and IT	Large enterprises with strong data domains
Hybrid	Central strategy + distributed execution	Most common; balances control and agility

Start with a lightweight version, then evolve as your governance matures.

3. Define Core Roles and Responsibilities

Clear roles are the foundation of accountability. Use a RACI (Responsible, Accountable, Consulted, Informed) matrix to avoid overlaps and gaps.

Role	Responsibilities
Data Owner	Accountable for data quality, access, and usage within a domain (e.g., finance)
Data Steward	Maintains data quality, definitions, and issue resolution day-to-day
Data Custodian	Technical role responsible for storing and securing data (often IT)
Data Governance Council	Approves policies, resolves conflicts, prioritises initiatives
Executive Sponsor	Champions programme, removes roadblocks, ensures funding and visibility

Document and communicate these roles clearly. People support what they understand.

4. Establish Guiding Principles

Governance should not feel arbitrary. Define principles to guide decision-making. Examples:

- Data is a strategic asset
- Everyone is a data citizen
- Governance should enable, not block, innovation

- Data should be governed at the point of creation
- Quality, security, and privacy are shared responsibilities

These help reinforce the **why** of governance during implementation.

5. **Define Policies and Standards**

   Start with a minimal, high-impact set of governance policies:

   - **Data Ownership Policy:** Who owns what, and what that means
   - **Data Quality Policy:** Acceptable thresholds and who remediates
   - **Data Access & Security Policy:** Who can see/use what and how it is approved
   - **Metadata & Lineage Policy:** What metadata must be captured and why
   - **Master Data Management Policy:** Standards for reference/master domains

Each policy should be:

- Short (1–2 pages)
- Written in plain language
- Aligned with existing risk/compliance standards

6. **Set Up Governance Processes**

   Processes operationalise your framework. Start with:

Process	Purpose
Issue Management	Identify, log, assign, and resolve data quality issues
Change Requests	Review and approve proposed changes to key data definitions
Policy Exception Review	Evaluate requests to override governance standards
Stewardship Forums	Regular reviews of domain-level quality, usage, and issues
Governance Council	Strategic alignment and decision-making

Define SLAs and escalation paths. Governance must be responsive to be respected.

7. Align with Technology — Don't Over-Engineer

Your framework should inform — not be constrained by — your tools. Select tools that support:

- Data lineage and cataloguing (e.g., Collibra, Alation)
- Quality monitoring (e.g., Informatica, Talend)
- Metadata management
- Policy enforcement (e.g., through data platforms or API layers)

But do not let tools dictate your structure. Process first. Tools second.

8. Document and Communicate the Framework

Once your framework is defined:

- Create a visual diagram showing the governance operating model
- Draft a Data Governance Charter: A concise document outlining purpose, scope, roles, and principles
- Publish FAQs and one-pagers for business units
- Conduct a launch event or workshop

Governance frameworks fail in the dark. Make yours visible and approachable.

Checklist: Governance Framework Essentials

- ✓ Selected an appropriate governance model
- ✓ Defined clear roles and accountabilities
- ✓ Established principles, policies, and standards
- ✓ Designed key governance processes
- ✓ Mapped tool support (where applicable)
- ✓ Communicated the framework across the organisation

Up Next

Chapter 5 – Establishing Roles: Owners, Stewards, and Councils

Now that your governance framework is taking shape, it's time to bring it to life through people. In Chapter 5, we'll dive into the essential roles that make governance real — from data owners and stewards to custodians and governance councils.

You'll learn how to assign responsibilities with clarity, avoid role confusion, and activate the human engine behind your data strategy. Because frameworks may define the structure — but it's people who make governance work.

Establishing Roles: Owners, Stewards, and Councils

"Governance is not a software project. It is a people project."

At the heart of every successful data governance programme is a network of empowered, accountable individuals. This chapter focuses on how to define, assign, and activate the human structure of your governance framework — turning job descriptions into real action.

1. Why Roles Matter

Many organisations write beautiful governance policies that fail in practice because no one knows who is actually responsible. Defining roles brings clarity, accountability, and consistency. It also:

- Prevents duplication and confusion
- Clarifies decision rights
- Accelerates issue resolution
- Increases adoption of standards

Think of your governance structure like a relay race — if no one owns the baton at any point, you lose.

2. The Core Governance Roles

Let us break down the essential players and their typical responsibilities:

A. Data Owners

Who they are: Typically, senior business leaders (e.g., Head of Finance, CMO, COO)

Key responsibilities:
- Own the quality, security, and usage of data in their domain
- Approve data definitions and standards
- Escalate or resolve cross-functional conflicts
- Champion governance within their teams

Selection tip: Choose leaders with both authority and accountability for how data is used — not just how it's stored.

B. Data Stewards

Who they are: Subject-matter experts embedded in business functions (e.g., billing analysts, claims processors, CRM managers)

Key responsibilities:
- Maintain data definitions and quality rules
- Monitor and report on data quality issues
- Serve as the first line of support for governance processes
- Collaborate with IT and custodians on system updates and changes

Selection tip: Look for people who already informally "own" data — they often become natural stewards.

C. Data Custodians

Who they are: IT or system administrators

Key responsibilities:
- Ensure systems align with governance policies
- Implement access controls, backups, and security
- Collaborate with owners/stewards to enforce data quality standards

Selection tip: Align with infrastructure, security, and architecture teams early.

D. Data Governance Council

Who they are: Cross-functional leadership group (business + IT + risk/compliance)

Key responsibilities:
- Provide strategic oversight and prioritisation
- Approve policies and resolve escalated issues
- Monitor progress and enforce accountability
- Ensure alignment with organisational strategy

Structure tip: Start with monthly meetings. Assign a chair and a charter.

E. Governance Operating Team

Who they are: Programme leads, data governance managers, data architects

Key responsibilities:
- Run the day-to-day governance initiative
- Track KPIs, prepare dashboards, coordinate projects
- Deliver training and communications

Structure tip: This is your execution engine. They keep things moving.

3. Assigning and Activating Roles

Once roles are defined, the next step is to assign them in a way that works. Follow these steps:

1. Map your domains (e.g., customer, finance, product, supplier, HR)
2. Identify potential owners in each domain based on decision-making authority
3. Engage them directly with a short role description and invitation
4. Pilot in 1–2 domains before expanding
5. Formally document assignments in a RACI matrix or registry

Pro tip: Make role onboarding easy — use a simple 1-pager for each role with:
- Key responsibilities
- Reporting lines
- Tools used
- First 30-day actions

4. Embed Governance into Job Roles

The most sustainable governance programmes embed responsibilities into existing roles and performance reviews. Consider:

- Updating job descriptions to include data stewardship duties
- Aligning with HR to include data quality in KPIs
- Recognising stewards/owners in performance discussions

Incentives matter. Even a "Steward of the Month" spotlight can go a long way in reinforcing culture.

5. Provide Tools and Training

New roles need support. Equip your data community with:

- Role-specific training (e.g., Collibra, Purview, Excel-based DQ tracking)
- Playbooks for common tasks (e.g., updating definitions, resolving duplicates)
- Communities of practice or governance forums
- Office hours or coaching with the governance team

This is not just change management — it is culture change.

Checklist: Establishing Roles

- ✓ Defined and documented governance roles
- ✓ Mapped data domains and candidate owners/stewards
- ✓ Assigned roles with clarity and authority
- ✓ Created onboarding materials and playbooks
- ✓ Provided tooling, training, and support
- ✓ Embedded responsibilities into HR and performance processes

Up Next

Chapter 6 – Policies, Standards, and Procedures: From Paper to Practice

With your people activated and your framework in place, it is time to turn policy into practice. In Chapter 6, we will guide you through writing practical data governance policies, developing enforceable standards, and embedding procedures that actually get followed.

Chapter 6

Policies, Standards, and Procedures – From Paper to Practice

"Policies do not govern data. People following policies do."

One of the most common pitfalls in data governance is the creation of thick, unreadable policy documents that sit unused on shared drives. The real value of governance policies lies not in their existence but in their ***adoption and enforcement***. This chapter shows how to create clear, usable policies, standards, and procedures that embed governance into your organisation's daily operations.

1. Clarify the Difference: Policy vs. Standard vs. Procedure

Understanding the hierarchy is essential:

- **Policy** – High-level rules that define ***what*** must be done (e.g., "All data domains must have an assigned owner.")
- **Standard** – Specific technical or business criteria that define ***how*** data should conform (e.g., "Customer names must be stored in [First Name, Last Name] format.")
- **Procedure** – Step-by-step actions to enforce policies and meet standards (e.g., "Steps for requesting a new customer record in the CRM system.")

All three must work together — policy defines intent, standards define consistency, and procedures define action.

2. Characteristics of Good Governance Policies

Effective data governance policies share these traits:

- **Clear** – Avoid jargon. Aim for simplicity and brevity.
- **Actionable** – Assign accountability. Policies should not be theoretical.

- **Relevant** – Tie policies to business objectives and regulatory needs.
- **Accessible** – Easily found, read, and understood by staff.
- **Endorsed** – Formally approved by the governance council and communicated widely.

Structure tip: Keep policies to 1–2 pages and use consistent headings like:

- Purpose
- Scope
- Policy Statement
- Responsibilities
- Exceptions
- Enforcement

3. Core Policies to Prioritise

Start with a small set of foundational policies that directly impact governance maturity and data risk:

Policy Name	Description
Data Ownership Policy	Defines who owns which data and their responsibilities
Data Quality Policy	Sets minimum quality thresholds and outlines resolution rules
Access & Security Policy	Defines access controls, roles, and data classification rules
Metadata Policy	Outlines expectations for data definitions and lineage
Master Data Policy	Establishes rules for managing shared reference/master data

Don't create policies you can't enforce. Start with what matters most.

4. Develop Practical Standards

Data standards promote consistency across systems and processes. Focus on:

- Naming conventions (e.g., no special characters, consistent abbreviations)

- Data formats (e.g., date formats: YYYY-MM-DD)
- Validation rules (e.g., mandatory fields like email or customer ID)
- Classification tiers (e.g., Public, Internal, Confidential, Restricted)

Use a Data Standards Catalogue stored in a central location — ideally within a metadata tool or SharePoint site.

Tip: Work with business users when developing standards to avoid unworkable technical rules.

5. Define Repeatable Procedures

Procedures operationalise your policies. Prioritise common and high-risk activities such as:

- Submitting and resolving a data quality issue
- Requesting access to sensitive data
- Creating or modifying a data definition
- Approving and onboarding a new data owner or steward
- Requesting a change to master/Reference Data

Keep procedures visual and short. Use:

- Flowcharts
- Step-by-step instructions
- Embedded links to request forms or tools

Example: Procedure to Request Access to Customer Data

1. Submit access request via internal portal
2. Owner receives automated alert and reviews
3. Approve or reject request within 3 working days
4. Custodian applies access in system
5. Requester receives confirmation email

6. Communicate and Train

The best-written policy still fails if no one knows it exists. For each policy:

- Publish it on a central governance hub (intranet, SharePoint, Confluence)
- Run a short policy onboarding session with key teams
- Create bite-sized explainer videos or FAQs
- Include policies in data stewardship training
- Reference policies during quality reviews and audits

Tip: Start with a "Policy of the Month" spotlight to avoid overwhelming teams.

7. **Monitor Compliance and Revise Periodically**

   Policies and standards must evolve with your business. Create a cadence to:
   - Review and update policies every 6–12 months
   - Collect feedback from stewards and owners
   - Monitor exceptions and violations
   - Track adoption using KPIs (e.g., # of issues resolved per procedure, % of data domains with active owners)

Enforcement should be supportive, not punitive — focus on education and enablement.

Checklist: From Paper to Practice

- ✓ Defined the difference between policy, standard, and procedure
- ✓ Created 3–5 high-impact governance policies
- ✓ Developed standards for data naming, formatting, and classification
- ✓ Documented step-by-step procedures for common governance actions
- ✓ Communicated policies widely and included them in onboarding
- ✓ Set a review schedule to keep policies relevant and effective

Up Next

Chapter 7 – Data Quality as a Cornerstone

With the right people and policies in place, the next challenge is execution. In Chapter 7, we will explore how to define, measure, and improve data quality — and why trust in data is the foundation of every successful governance programme.

Chapter 7

Data Quality as a Cornerstone

"If you cannot trust the data, you cannot trust the decision."

Data governance is ultimately about trust — and trust begins with quality. No matter how elegant your governance framework is, it will fail if your data is inaccurate, incomplete, inconsistent, or outdated. In this chapter, we'll break down what data quality really means, how to measure it, and how to build a sustainable, business-led approach to improving it.

1. What Is Data Quality?

Data quality refers to the fitness of data for its intended use. It's not about technical perfection, but about reliability, usability, and value in context.

The DAMA-DMBOK and industry best practices define six core dimensions:

Dimension	Description
Accuracy	Is the data correct and reflective of reality?
Completeness	Are all required values present?
Consistency	Is the data uniform across systems and sources?
Timeliness	Is the data available when needed and up to date?
Validity	Does the data conform to required formats, rules, and standards?
Uniqueness	Are there duplicates or multiple versions of the same data entity?

You do not need to track every dimension for every dataset — prioritise based on business needs.

2. Make Data Quality a Business-Led Conversation

Too often, data quality is treated as an IT clean-up job. This approach misses the point: quality is defined by the people who use the data.

Here is how to make it business-led:

- Involve business units in defining what "good" looks like
- Let data stewards own issue logging and resolution
- Tie quality rules to specific use cases (e.g., marketing campaigns, regulatory filings)
- Communicate the impact of poor data in dollars, not just defects

Example:

"Due to inconsistent product codes, our Q1 procurement report double-counted £1.2M in inventory — causing budget rework and reputational harm."

3. Build a Data Quality Framework

A scalable approach to data quality includes these components:

1. **Data Quality Rules** – Logical conditions that define what is acceptable (e.g., "Customer email must not be blank")
2. **Data Quality KPIs** – Metrics to track overall health and progress (e.g., % of complete records)
3. **Issue Management Process** – A workflow for identifying, assigning, and resolving issues
4. **Monitoring Tools** – Dashboards or platforms to automate and track checks
5. **Continuous Improvement Loop** – Regular review and refinement of rules and practices

Use a Data Quality Scorecard per domain to make insights visible and actionable.

4. Identify and Prioritise Critical Data Elements (CDEs)

Trying to measure quality across all data is overwhelming. Focus on Critical Data Elements — high-impact data fields essential to operations, compliance, or analytics.

Examples of CDEs:

- Customer ID
- Invoice date
- Product SKU
- Policy number
- KYC attributes (e.g., birthdate, nationality)

Criteria for selection:

- Used in key business processes
- Required for external reporting
- Frequently queried or reconciled
- Prone to errors or inconsistencies

Prioritise 10–20 CDEs per domain to start.

5. Define and Apply Quality Rules

For each CDE, define data quality rules that reflect business needs. Examples:

CDE Rule	Description	Dimension
Customer Email	Must not be null and must match a valid email format	Validity
Invoice Date	Must be within the last 90 days	Timeliness
Product Code	Must follow "ABC-123" format	Consistency
Policy Number	Must be unique across system	Uniqueness

Rules can be monitored via tools like Informatica, Collibra, Ataccama, or even in Excel for smaller organisations.

6. Set Up Issue Management Workflows

When issues are found, how are they handled?

1. **Log** – Steward or user submits an issue (e.g., duplicate record, incorrect data)
2. **Classify** – Categorise by severity, impact, and domain

3. **Assign** – Route to appropriate steward, owner, or IT team
4. **Resolve** – Fix the issue and document root cause
5. **Close** – Validate, fix, and update audit trail

Track resolution time, root cause patterns, and recurring issues.

7. Use Metrics to Track Progress and Build Confidence

Common data quality KPIs:

- % of records meeting all quality rules
- Issues opened/closed per month
- Mean time to resolve (MTTR)
- % of CDEs with assigned data stewards
- Business satisfaction (via surveys or NPS)

Visual dashboards can help sustain executive attention and cross-functional momentum.

8. Embed Data Quality into Daily Operations

For long-term success, data quality must move from project to process:

- Include DQ reviews in monthly governance forums
- Integrate DQ rules into ETL, CRM, and ERP processes
- Make DQ a step in new data onboarding
- Recognise and reward teams that improve data quality

Tip: Quality culture thrives when users see visible improvement in their day-to-day work.

Checklist: Making Data Quality Real

- ✓ Defined 5–6 data quality dimensions aligned to business needs
- ✓ Identified high-impact Critical Data Elements
- ✓ Created business-led data quality rules
- ✓ Set up issue logging and resolution workflows

✓ Measured and reported quality through KPIs and dashboards

✓ Embedded data quality into operational routines

Up Next

Chapter 8 – Metadata Management and Data Catalogues

Data quality tells you whether your data is usable — but metadata tells you what the data means. In Chapter 8, we will explore how to manage metadata, build data catalogues, and create a shared language across your organisation.

⊷⊶

Metadata Management and Data Catalogues

"You cannot govern what you do not understand — and that is what metadata is for."

Metadata is the foundation of transparency in data governance. It tells us what data we have, where it lives, how it moves, and what it means. Without strong metadata management, organisations struggle with duplication, confusion, and mistrust. In this chapter, we explore how to create a robust metadata strategy and leverage data catalogues to make your data visible, searchable, and governable.

1. What Is Metadata?

Metadata is **"data about data"**. It provides context — enabling users to interpret, trust, and use data accurately.

There are three core types of metadata:

Type	Description
Business Metadata	Business definitions, policies, data stewards, ownership info
Technical Metadata	Table names, columns, data types, file paths, storage formats
Operational Metadata	Data lineage, frequency of updates, data quality stats

Example:

For a field called Customer_ID, metadata would describe:

- What it represents (business metadata)
- Where it lives in the database (technical metadata)

- How it flows between systems and how often it's updated (operational metadata)

2. Why Metadata Matters for Governance

Good metadata management:

- Enables data discovery and reuse
- Reduces duplication and redundancy
- Supports data lineage for compliance and audit
- Clarifies data ownership and usage permissions
- Helps users understand the meaning and relevance of data

Think of metadata as the glue that binds your data governance framework together.

3. Build a Metadata Management Strategy

To govern metadata effectively, organisations must:

- Define a metadata model: What fields are collected and why?
- Assign metadata responsibilities to stewards and owners
- Establish metadata standards (naming conventions, definitions, tags)
- Integrate metadata into daily workflows and governance processes

Start with what matters most: High-priority domains, frequently accessed datasets, and regulatory-critical fields.

4. Implement a Data Catalogue

A data catalogue is a centralised platform that helps users:

- Search and discover data assets
- Understand definitions and lineage
- Identify ownership and usage policies
- Collaborate through annotations, ratings, and comments

Popular tools include:

- Collibra
- Alation

- Microsoft Purview
- Informatica Axon
- Atlan

Open-source: Amundsen, DataHub, Metacat

Tip: Don't aim for 100% coverage from the start — begin with 1–2 domains and scale.

5. Metadata Collection Approaches

There are three key methods to populate your catalogue:

Method	Pros	Cons
Manual Entry	• High control, useful for business definitions	• Time-consuming • Hard to scale
Automated Scanning	• Scalable for technical metadata	• May miss business context • Depends on tools
Crowdsourcing	• Engages users • Captures tribal knowledge	• Quality control can be inconsistent

The best approach is hybrid — use automated scanning for technical lineage and empower stewards to enrich business metadata.

6. Define Metadata Standards

Develop standards to ensure consistency. Examples:

- Table and column naming conventions (e.g., use underscores, avoid abbreviations)
- Standard formats for dates, currency, IDs
- Required fields in metadata (e.g., Owner, Description, Last Updated)
- Classification tags (e.g., PII, Sensitive, Public)

Publish your standards and enforce them in new project reviews and onboarding processes.

7. Connect Metadata to Other Governance Domains

Metadata is not just for IT. Make it central to other governance processes:

- **Data quality**: Show linked rules, thresholds, and issues per field
- **Access control:** Define usage restrictions and sensitivity levels
- **Master data**: Indicate golden record sources and linkages
- **Lineage and compliance:** Visualise data flow for audit and impact analysis

This integration makes metadata actionable, not just decorative.

8. Drive Engagement and Adoption

To keep your Catalogue from becoming a "ghost town":

- Promote it through internal training, lunch-and-learns, or demos
- Include metadata usage in data stewardship KPIs
- Allow users to comment, suggest edits, and request clarifications
- Highlight "Featured Datasets" or "Trusted Sources" monthly
- Celebrate adoption milestones across teams

People use what they trust — and trust what is up-to-date and accessible.

Checklist: Metadata and Catalogue Success

- ✓ Defined metadata types and scope for key data assets
- ✓ Selected or deployed a user-friendly data catalogue
- ✓ Automated technical metadata scanning for key systems
- ✓ Assigned metadata stewardship and trained staff
- ✓ Created standards for naming, tagging, and classification
- ✓ Integrated metadata with quality, access, and lineage processes
- ✓ Promoted usage and captured feedback from the business

Up Next

Chapter 9 – Master and Reference Data: Getting Your Core Data Right

Even the best metadata and quality programmes crumble without consistent core data. In Chapter 9, we'll dive into master and Reference Data management (MDM/RDM) — why it matters, how to design a golden record strategy, and how to avoid common MDM pitfalls.

Master and Reference Data — Getting Your Core Data Right

"If your foundation is cracked, no amount of polish will help."

Master and Reference Data are the backbone of your organisation's information landscape. Without consistent and governed core data — like customer IDs, product codes, country lists, or chart of accounts — even the most sophisticated analytics or reporting solutions will fail. This chapter explains how to govern master and Reference Data effectively, and why it's critical to enterprise data governance success.

1. What Is Master Data?

Master Data refers to non-transactional data that represents the key business entities an organisation relies on.

Examples include:

- Customers
- Products
- Suppliers
- Employees
- Locations
- Accounts

Master Data is often used across systems and departments, which is why inconsistency causes wide-reaching issues — from CRM and billing mismatches to regulatory reporting errors.

2. What Is Reference Data?

Reference Data is a subset of master data that defines allowable values for a given field or domain.

Examples include:

- Country or currency codes (e.g., "NGN", "USD")
- Product categories (e.g., "Electronics", "Appliances")
- Risk ratings
- Gender or marital status codes
- VAT classifications

Poor Reference Data governance leads to:

- Invalid transactions
- Regulatory misclassification
- System integration failures
- Confusion in reporting or decision-making

3. Why Master & Reference Data Go Wrong

The most common problems:

- Multiple versions of the truth (e.g., duplicate customer IDs)
- Local variations without alignment (e.g., region-specific category names)
- Lack of ownership for central entities
- Inconsistent standards across applications
- Manual entry and free text fields without validation

These issues result in rework, disputes, operational risk, and reputational damage.

4. Build a Master Data Governance Framework

Start small, but establish a structured approach:

Component	Description
Data Domains	Identify which entities need to be governed (start with 1–2)
Golden Record Rules	Define how the "single source of truth" is created and validated
Stewardship	Assign business stewards to maintain and update records
Data Standards	Format, naming, and business rules (e.g., mandatory fields, code lists)
Survivorship Logic	Rules for resolving duplicates or conflicts
Integration Strategy	Define how systems consume and update MDM sources

Tip: Make sure golden records are fit-for-purpose. There's no need to consolidate all data into a single system unless the use case demands it.

5. Choose the Right MDM Operating Model

There are different ways to implement Master Data Management (MDM), depending on your structure and systems.

Model Description	Best For
Registry Metadata-driven directory; no physical data movement	• Quick wins • Minimal disruption
Consolidation Central hub creates golden records from multiple sources	• Analytics • Reporting harmonisation
Coexistence Golden records are created but updates happen in source systems	• Large organisations with decentralised ownership
Centralised One master system creates and distributes all updates	• Heavily regulated or integrated businesses

Start with a use case, not a tool.

6. Apply Governance to Reference Data

Reference Data is often overlooked — yet it touches almost every system. Best practices include:

- Centralised stewardship or governance board
- Standard naming, description, and classification rules
- Controlled change management for adding or retiring values
- Version control and effective communication to users
- Integration with downstream systems to prevent invalid values

Example:

"Inconsistent country codes led to a $500,000 tax reporting error due to incorrect classification of offshore transactions."

Reference Data is low volume, high impact — manage it with the same care as master data.

7. Leverage MDM Tools — But Only After You Define the Process

Popular MDM tools include:

- Informatica MDM
- Semarchy
- Reltio
- Profisee
- SAP MDG
- Microsoft Purview (for Reference Data)
- Talend MDM
- IBM InfoSphere

However, don't start with the tool. First define:

- Who owns the data
- What the business rules are
- What systems need to consume the data
- How data will be maintained and synchronised

Process before platform is the golden rule.

8. Monitor Quality and Usage

Even golden records degrade without care. Monitor:

- of duplicate records detected and resolved
- % of master records missing critical fields
- Timeliness of steward updates
- Data synchronisation success rate across systems
- Business usage and feedback

Add alerts or dashboards to flag exceptions and data decay early.

Checklist: Master & Reference Data Control

- ✓ Identified priority master data domains and reference lists
- ✓ Assigned owners and stewards to manage golden records
- ✓ Defined data standards and survivorship rules
- ✓ Implemented Reference Data governance workflows
- ✓ Chose MDM approach based on real business needs
- ✓ Built dashboards or reports to monitor accuracy and use

Up Next

Chapter 10 – Tooling and Technology: Enabling Governance Without Overkill

Data governance is not a tool — but the right tools make everything easier. In Chapter 10, we will explore how to choose governance tools wisely, integrate them with your ecosystem, and avoid common technology traps.

❡❡❡

Tooling and Technology – Enabling Governance Without Overkill

"Technology enables governance — it does not define it."

Many organisations fall into the trap of assuming that buying a data governance tool equals having a data governance programme. In reality, no platform can substitute for leadership, process, and accountability. However, the right tools — when introduced at the right time — can streamline workflows, increase visibility, and automate enforcement. This chapter helps you identify which technologies to prioritise, how to evaluate them, and how to integrate them meaningfully into your governance strategy.

1. Tooling Should Follow Process — Not the Other Way Around

Before choosing any platform, ensure you have already defined:

- Roles and responsibilities (owners, stewards, custodians)
- Business goals (e.g., better reporting, regulatory compliance)
- Use cases (e.g., improving customer data, streamlining product hierarchies)
- Governance workflows (e.g., issue resolution, metadata approvals)

Golden rule: Don't let tools shape your governance. Use your governance needs to shape the tool selection.

2. Categories of Data Governance Tools

Here are the core categories and what they support:

Tool Type	Key Capabilities
Metadata Management & Catalogues	Business glossary, Technical lineage, Data discovery

Tool Type	Key Capabilities
Data Quality Platforms	Profiling, Rule definition, Anomaly detection, Scorecards
Master & Reference Data Management (MDM/RDM)	Golden records, Hierarchy management, Code list control
Policy & Workflow Management	Approval processes, Stewardship dashboards, Policy lifecycle tracking
Access & Security Tools	Role-based access, PII classification, policy-based controls
Integration & Automation Tools	ETL/ELT pipelines, Data orchestration, Validation at ingestion points

3. Leading Tools in the Market (2025)

Category	Common Vendors
Catalogue/Metadata	Collibra, Alation, Microsoft Purview, Atlan, DataGalaxy, Informatica Axon
Data Quality	Informatica IDQ, Talend, Ataccama, SAS DQ, Monte Carlo, Bigeye, Soda
MDM & RDM	Reltio, Semarchy, Informatica MDM, SAP MDG, Profisee, IBM InfoSphere
Governance Platforms	OvalEdge, Solidatus, Precisely, erwin DI, Informatica Axon
Open-Source Options	Amundsen, DataHub, OpenMetadata, Metacat (for lightweight implementations)

Tip: Most tools now offer cloud-native, API-first, and AI-assisted functionality — but always focus on usability, not just features.

4. Key Capabilities to Look For

When evaluating tools, prioritise:

- Usability for business users (search, glossary, UI)
- Collaboration features (comments, requests, steward workflows)

- Integration with existing systems (data warehouses, BI, ETL)
- Automation of metadata harvesting, quality checks, notifications
- Lineage and impact analysis (especially for regulated environments)

Always pilot with a real use case (e.g., customer data governance) to assess actual value.

5. How to Introduce Tools in a Low-Risk Way

You do not need a "big bang" rollout. Consider this phased approach:

Phase 1: Pilot Use Case

- Define a narrow scope (e.g., product data catalogue)
- Onboard 1–2 teams
- Track early success metrics

Phase 2: Expand to Additional Domains

- Ingest more metadata
- Involve additional data stewards and SMEs
- Align dashboards and workflows to the council

Phase 3: Enterprise Rollout

- Integrate with data pipelines
- Standardise glossary and tagging conventions
- Embed tools into daily operations and training

Avoid launching a tool without a strong enablement and training plan.

6. Common Mistakes to Avoid

- Buying before aligning — purchasing tools before governance processes are mature
- Over-configuring — trying to automate or enforce every nuance at once
- IT-only ownership — without business engagement, tools go unused
- Neglecting adoption — no rollout plan, no champions, no training

- Focusing on breadth over depth — populating thousands of assets without quality metadata

Always keep tools tied to real business problems and steward engagement.

7. Make Tools a Part of Your Data Culture

To sustain adoption:

- Appoint platform champions or "data tool evangelists"
- Include tools in all governance onboarding and training
- Integrate catalogues into self-service analytics workflows
- Add tool usage metrics to your governance dashboards

The more people see value from a tool, the more they will engage with governance itself.

Checklist: Technology Readiness for Governance

- ✓ Defined governance needs and key use cases
- ✓ Evaluated tools based on integration, usability, and automation
- ✓ Piloted a tool with a real business domain
- ✓ Trained stewards, owners, and analysts
- ✓ Established phased rollout with KPIs
- ✓ Monitored tool adoption and engagement metrics

Up Next

Chapter 11 – Driving Change: Communication, Training, and Adoption

Technology and frameworks are only part of the puzzle. In Chapter 11, we will turn to people — how to engage them, train them, and drive the cultural change required for long-term **governance success.**

Driving Change – Communication, Training, and Adoption

"People do not resist governance — they resist confusion, complexity, and control without purpose."

Even the best-designed data governance initiative will stall if people do not understand it, believe in it, or know how to act on it. Change does not happen through policies alone — it happens through communication, behaviour shifts, and sustained engagement. In this chapter, we will unpack how to foster a culture of data accountability by equipping, engaging, and empowering your people.

1. Governance Is a Change Management Challenge

Governance requires new behaviours:

- Taking ownership of data
- Following defined standards and policies
- Logging and resolving issues consistently
- Trusting shared definitions instead of local variations

This is a cultural shift — and like all change, it must be led, reinforced, and normalised over time.

2. Build a Clear, Compelling Narrative

Governance must feel relevant. Anchor your messaging in pain points and benefits that resonate.

Avoid: *"We are launching a metadata management initiative with centralised stewardship workflows."*

Use: *"We are improving how customer data is managed so we can reduce reporting errors, deliver more accurate marketing, and avoid compliance risks."*

Craft a "governance elevator pitch" that answers:

- Why now?
- What is changing?
- Who is involved?
- What are the benefits?
- How can you help?

Make this your North Star in every communication.

3. Segment Your Audiences

Tailor your messaging for different stakeholders:

Audience	What They Care About	Messaging Focus
Executives	Risk, ROI, Brand, Regulation	Strategic alignment and KPIs
Data Owners	Accountability, Efficiency	Clear role definitions, Issue resolution
Data Stewards	Practical tools, Training, Support	Hands-on enablement and peer examples
IT & Architecture	Systems alignment, Automation	Integration points and control mechanisms
End Users	Relevance, Usability, Trust	Day-to-day impact and self-service access

Do not mass-email governance updates. Craft role-specific messages.

4. Launch a Governance Communication Plan

Use a multi-channel strategy to reinforce key messages consistently:

Channel	Example Use Case
Town Halls	Introduce governance vision and success stories
Intranet Page	Central hub for glossary, FAQs, policies, and tools

Channel	Example Use Case
Email Newsletters	Monthly updates, featured datasets, steward spotlights
Video	Shorts 2-minute explainers on governance concepts
Yammer/Teams/Slack	Live Q&A, stewardship discussions, governance wins
Business Unit Briefings	Domain-specific updates and training

Consistency builds credibility. Visibility builds trust.

5. Train for Capability and Confidence

Governance adoption requires skills — not just awareness.

Create training tailored by role:

- **For Stewards:** Definitions, DQ tools, issue logging, metadata management
- **For Owners:** Accountability, decision-making, policy review
- **For Analysts:** How to find, trust, and use governed data
- **For IT:** Integration with governance workflows, policy enforcement

Formats:

- Live workshops or virtual webinars
- Interactive eLearning modules
- Quick reference guides and videos
- Role-based onboarding packs

Tip: Do not train once. Create a recurring learning loop with refreshers and advanced sessions.

6. Identify and Empower Champions

Champions amplify adoption. Recruit and equip:

- **Data Evangelists:** Early adopters who promote governance within teams
- **Tool Superusers:** Stewards who support others in using the catalogue, DQ tools, etc.
- **Council Members:** Influencers who can escalate, support, and model behaviour

Recognise them publicly. Give them first access to updates. Include them in decision feedback loops.

7. Create Rituals that Reinforce Governance

Culture is sustained by repetition. Embed governance into everyday operations:

- Add DQ metrics to monthly ops reviews
- Review glossary terms during sprint planning
- Spotlight stewards in team meetings
- Include governance KPIs in performance dashboards
- Share monthly "Data Wins" (e.g., duplicate reduction, faster onboarding)

Governance should feel like part of "how we work" — not an add-on.

8. Track Engagement and Adjust

Use metrics to gauge adoption:

- Training completion rates
- Catalogue/tool usage stats
- Number of issues logged and resolved
- Feedback surveys on usefulness of governance processes
- Participation in governance forums

Adapt your approach based on what works — and what is being ignored.

Checklist: Driving Governance Adoption

- ✓ Defined a clear narrative for "why governance now"
- ✓ Tailored communication and training by role
- ✓ Established a multi-channel comms strategy
- ✓ Created role-specific training content and rituals
- ✓ Identified and empowered governance champions
- ✓ Monitored engagement and feedback for continuous improvement

Up Next

Chapter 12 – Measuring Impact: KPIs and Continuous Improvement

You cannot manage what you do not measure. In Chapter 12, we will explore how to define success, track it over time, and continuously refine your data governance programme for greater business value.

⸺◈⸺

Chapter 12

Measuring Impact – KPIs and Continuous Improvement

"If data is an asset, governance is how we protect and grow its value. But value must be measured to be sustained."

The ultimate test of your data governance programme is not how many policies are written or how many stewards are trained — it is how much value the programme creates for the business. Measuring impact allows you to sustain investment, improve performance, and evolve your governance model. This chapter gives you the practical tools and KPIs to track success and build a culture of continuous improvement.

1. Why Measurement Matters

Without measurement:

- Leadership won't stay engaged
- Stakeholders won't see the value
- Teams won't know what's working
- Priorities drift, and momentum slows

With measurement:

- You can justify investment and scale governance
- You can reward progress and spotlight champions
- You can course-correct early and often

Governance is not a set-and-forget initiative. It must mature with the business - and that requires feedback.

2. Define What "Success" Means for Your Organisation

Start by aligning your KPIs with your original business case. Ask:

- What were we trying to solve?
- What did we promise would improve?
- What value are we trying to unlock - or protect?

Your measurement strategy should include:

- Compliance metrics
- Operational efficiency gains
- Risk reduction indicators
- Data quality improvements
- User satisfaction and adoption trends

3. Structure Your KPIs Across 4 Levels

Level	What It Measures	Examples
Strategic KPIs	Alignment with enterprise goals	% of regulatory deadlines met, audit pass rate
Operational KPIs	Governance process performance	Issue resolution time, % of policies implemented
Data Quality KPIs	Accuracy, Completeness, Consistency	% of records passing all quality rules
Engagement KPIs	User adoption and participation	Catalogue usage, Training completion, Steward activity

A strong measurement framework includes a few indicators from each category.

4. Practical Examples of Data Governance KPIs

Data Quality

- % of critical data elements (CDEs) that meet quality thresholds
- Number of duplicate records reduced per month
- Number of data issues logged vs. resolved

Policy & Process

- % of domains with assigned data owners/stewards
- % of governance policies reviewed and approved
- of governance council meetings held with quorum

Engagement & Usage

- of catalogue searches per month
- of glossary terms reviewed or added
- % of teams using governed reports or assets

Strategic Outcomes

- Reduction in reporting cycle time
- Reduction in regulatory fines or audit issues
- Time saved on reconciliations or duplicate clean-ups

5. Create a Data Governance Dashboard

Build a dashboard or scorecard that includes:

- Visual KPIs (bar, trend, heatmap)
- Domain-specific breakdowns (e.g., customer vs. product data)
- Targets and thresholds (e.g., 90% quality score)
- Owner accountability (e.g., by steward or business function)
- Change over time (month-on-month or quarter-on-quarter)

Tools to consider: Power BI, Tableau, Excel, Google Data Studio, or your governance platform's native dashboarding tools.

Make dashboards visible to:

- Governance council
- Business leadership
- Stewards and analysts

Transparency drives accountability.

6. Review, Reflect, and Refine

Schedule regular governance reviews:

- **Monthly:** Operational reviews (DQ issues, tool usage, metadata updates)
- **Quarterly:** Executive reviews (strategic KPIs, programme progress)
- **Annually:** Programme health check and roadmap refresh

Use the Plan → Do → Check → Act (PDCA) cycle:

- Plan: Define new goals or updates based on feedback
- Do: Implement policies, train teams, or enhance tools
- Check: Review metrics, audit outcomes, or adoption
- Act: Adjust course — double down on success, fix gaps

Make improvement part of your DNA.

7. Celebrate and Communicate Progress

Do not just track success — talk about it:

- Highlight progress in monthly newsletters
- Feature "Data Heroes" who solve tough problems
- Share before-and-after stories (e.g., duplicate clean-up success)
- Translate metrics into value (e.g., "Saved 120 hours per month")

Governance becomes real when people feel the impact — and see their role in creating it.

Checklist: Governance Measurement & Improvement

- ✓ Aligned KPIs to governance goals and business strategy
- ✓ Defined tiered metrics (strategic, operational, quality, engagement)
- ✓ Built a visual governance dashboard for tracking and reporting
- ✓ Scheduled regular reviews and PDCA cycles
- ✓ Publicised successes and engaged stakeholders with results
- ✓ Established a continuous improvement process

Up Next

Chapter 13 — Sector Deep Dives: Finance, Healthcare, Telecom, and Government

While the principles of governance are universal, how they're applied depends on your industry. In Chapter 13, we'll explore sector-specific use cases, challenges, and best practices — to help you tailor your governance programme to the realities of your domain.

———◆———

Chapter 13

Sector Deep Dives – Finance, Healthcare, Telecom, and Government

"Governance must be industry-aware — because context determines control."

Data governance is not one-size-fits-all. While the core principles remain constant, each sector brings its own challenges, regulations, data models, and expectations. In this chapter, we examine how governance plays out in four major industries — finance, healthcare, telecommunications, and government — and how to tailor your approach for maximum impact in each.

1. Finance: Accuracy, Auditability, and Risk

Why governance is critical:

- Regulatory frameworks like Basel III, BCBS 239, SOX, and GDPR
- High volume of sensitive data (KYC, credit, transactions)
- Demand for data lineage and traceability in reporting

Key governance priorities:

- Data lineage and traceability for audit and risk compliance
- Standardised Reference Data (currencies, accounts, counterparty IDs)
- Data quality controls embedded in financial reporting pipelines
- Master data management for customers, products, and instruments
- Metadata to support regulatory definitions and golden sources

Best practices:

- Integrate governance with risk and compliance teams
- Use data quality thresholds to gate key reporting cycles

- Leverage lineage tools to support regulatory data traceability
- Establish a Data Control Office to monitor reconciliation and remediation

KPI example:

% of regulatory submissions meeting internal data quality benchmarks

2. Healthcare: Privacy, Provenance, and Patient Safety

Why governance is critical:

- Strict compliance mandates (HIPAA, GDPR, HITECH)
- Highly sensitive data (PHI, EHR, lab results)
- Interoperability challenges across EMR/EHR systems
- Clinical decisions relying on high-trust data

Key governance priorities:

- Consent and access management for sensitive data
- Master data for patients, providers, medications, procedures
- Metadata to track provenance (e.g., source of diagnosis codes)
- Reference Data alignment (ICD-10, SNOMED, HL7 standards)
- Clear stewardship for clinical vs. administrative data

Best practices:

- Embed governance into electronic health record (EHR) workflows
- Collaborate with clinical data stewards, not just IT
- Automate metadata tagging for data coming from devices or labs
- Use data catalogues with privacy classification built-in

KPI example:

% of data access requests processed within consent boundaries and SLA

3. Telecommunications: Scale, Complexity, and Speed

Why governance is critical:

- Millions of customers, devices, and services

- Real-time data ingestion and monetisation (CDRs, location data, streaming)
- Evolving regulations (e.g., data sovereignty, consumer data rights)
- Complex BSS/OSS environments

Key governance priorities:

- Customer and service master data (SIM, devices, accounts)
- Metadata to support real-time usage monitoring and billing
- Data lineage across BSS/OSS, CRM, and DWH ecosystems
- Automated quality checks on real-time feeds
- Reference Data governance for plans, bundles, and product hierarchies

Best practices:

- Implement federated stewardship across network and commercial teams
- Create cross-functional data squads for shared domains (e.g., prepaid services)
- Ensure governance tools support high-volume, near-real-time datasets
- Integrate governance into data product lifecycle (e.g., new mobile plans)

KPI example:

% reduction in dropped or misbilled customer events after DQ rule enforcement

4. Government: Transparency, Public Trust, and Interagency Coordination

Why governance is critical:

- High public visibility and accountability
- Numerous departments with siloed data
- Legislative mandates for data sharing, privacy, and openness
- Legacy systems and resource constraints

Key governance priorities:
- Establishing common data standards across agencies
- Metadata for data inventories, classifications, and risk levels
- Clear stewardship models for open data vs. confidential data
- Policy governance for FOIA, GDPR, NDPR, or other compliance mandates
- Auditability and traceability of public-facing reports

Best practices:
- Start with high-value public datasets (e.g., health stats, census)
- Mandate metadata documentation before data publishing
- Use federated governance to allow agency-specific implementation
- Tie governance outcomes to citizen service delivery metrics

KPI example:

% of public datasets with complete metadata and data quality certifications

Common Cross-Sector Lessons

Despite their differences, all four sectors benefit from:
- Appointing domain-specific stewards
- Aligning governance goals with external and internal compliance obligations
- Investing in metadata and lineage to improve traceability and trust
- Embedding governance tools into operational and analytical workflows
- Measuring governance effectiveness through real-world outcomes

Checklist: Adapting Governance to Industry Context
- ✓ Identified sector-specific regulations and standards
- ✓ Defined critical data assets and domains unique to the industry
- ✓ Tailored stewardship and policy models to organisational structure

✓ Embedded governance into relevant workflows and tooling ecosystems

✓ Measured impact through sector-specific KPIs and audit results

Up Next

Chapter 14 – AI and the Future of Governance

As organisations race to adopt AI, the need for robust, ethical, and traceable data governance has never been more urgent. In Chapter 14, we'll explore how governance is evolving to meet the challenges of AI, machine learning, and data ethics in the modern enterprise.

❖

AI and the Future of Governance – Ethics, Risk, and Responsibility

"AI is only as ethical, accurate, and accountable as the data — and governance — behind it."

The rise of Artificial Intelligence and machine learning has elevated the role of data from a business asset to a strategic differentiator. Yet, as AI systems become more integrated into decision-making, the need for robust data governance multiplies — not just to ensure accuracy, but to safeguard fairness, transparency, and accountability. This chapter explores how traditional governance must evolve to meet the risks and opportunities of AI.

1. Why AI Raises the Stakes for Governance

AI systems rely on large datasets — often drawn from multiple domains, over long periods, and at great scale. Poor data governance can lead to:

- Bias in models due to skewed or incomplete training data
- Opaque decisions with no lineage or audit trail
- Data breaches from inadequate access control or classification
- Regulatory non-compliance with GDPR, NDPR, CCPA, and emerging AI-specific legislation

In short, AI amplifies the consequences of poor data.

2. Key Governance Challenges in the Age of AI

Challenge	Governance Implication
Data Bias	Need for source traceability, data diversity tracking
Model Explainability	Need for metadata on features, assumptions, training sets
Ethical Oversight	Clear policies on consent, data usage, and unintended impacts
Automated Decisions	Transparency, auditability, and human-in-the-loop governance
Dynamic Data	Versioning, Real-time monitoring, and Quality tracking

AI governance is not separate from data governance — it is the next frontier of it.

3. Extend Your Governance Framework for AI

To govern AI effectively, extend traditional data governance domains:

- **Metadata:** Track model inputs, training sets, owners, refresh cycles
- **Lineage:** Document the full lifecycle from source data to prediction
- **Quality:** Define thresholds for model data inputs (e.g., missing values)
- **Policy:** Draft ethical guidelines for automated decision-making
- **Stewardship:** Appoint AI model stewards for transparency and accountability
- **Monitoring:** Introduce bias audits, fairness checks, and model performance reviews

Tip: Treat models like data products — they require ownership, documentation, and lifecycle management.

4. Implement AI Governance Principles

Adopt principles aligned to globally emerging best practices, such as those from the EU AI Act, OECD, and ISO 42001:

Principle	Governance Mechanism
Transparency	Model cards, Explainability metadata, Lineage documentation
Accountability	Named model owners, Clear approval workflows
Fairness	Bias detection, Training set diversity checks
Privacy	Consent tracking, Data minimisation in features
Safety	Monitoring of outcomes, Risk scoring, Fallback protocols

Governance should not slow AI — it should ensure it is usable and safe.

5. Integrate AI into Your Governance Council

Evolve your data governance operating model to include:

- AI/ML Ethics Subcommittees
- Model Review Boards for high-impact use cases
- Risk scoring frameworks for AI projects
- Cross-functional representation from Legal, Risk, Compliance, and Data Science

Sample process:

1. Submit new model for governance review
2. Document inputs, assumptions, and intended use
3. Review against bias, privacy, and risk criteria
4. Log approval, monitoring plan, and owner accountability

This adds assurance — and protects reputation and compliance.

6. Tools Supporting AI Governance

Modern data governance platforms are expanding to support AI workflows:

- **Collibra AI Governance:** Tracks model metadata and approval workflows
- **Alation and Atlan:** Connect models to data assets via metadata
- **Truera and Fiddler AI:** Focused on bias, explainability, and monitoring
- **DataRobot MLOps and Azure ML:** Offer model lineage and drift tracking

- **Open-source:** Model Cards, MLFlow, and DataHub with AI metadata extensions

Evaluate integration based on your maturity and regulatory exposure.

7. Stay Ahead of AI Regulation

Regulations are evolving fast. Be prepared to demonstrate:

- Provenance of training data
- Risk classification of each AI system
- User consent and redress mechanisms
- Model documentation and auditability
- Human override or explanation options

The EU AI Act, U.S. Algorithmic Accountability Act, and NDPR AI guidelines are early examples — more are coming.

Checklist: AI-Ready Data Governance

- ✓ Extended governance framework to include AI/ML lifecycle
- ✓ Implemented model metadata, lineage, and documentation
- ✓ Established model stewardship and review boards
- ✓ Defined ethical and regulatory policy guidelines
- ✓ Adopted tools to support transparency and monitoring
- ✓ Aligned governance to current and emerging AI regulations

Conclusion: Your First 100 Days in Data Governance

Congratulations!

You now hold a blueprint for practical, scalable, and impactful data governance. But success lies not in reading, but in *acting*. In the final section of this book, we will lay out a 100-day roadmap to help you get started, gain momentum, and prove value fast — no matter your industry or maturity level.

CONCLUSION: YOUR FIRST 100 DAYS IN DATA GOVERNANCE
"Start small. Start smart. Start now."

You have now explored the full arc of designing and delivering a practical data governance programme — from understanding the foundations to executing at scale and adapting to the future. But the true test is this: *can you make it real in your organisation?*

You do not need perfection. You need progress.

That is why we conclude this book with a **practical 100-day roadmap** — a phased, momentum-building plan you can use to start (or reboot) governance efforts with credibility, clarity, and purpose.

THE 100-DAY DATA GOVERNANCE ROADMAP

Phase 1: Days 1–30 — Discover and Mobilise
Goal: Understand where you are, build support, and define your first use case.

Task	Output
Conduct a rapid governance maturity assessment	Summary of current strengths and gaps
Identify key stakeholders (IT, business, risk, compliance)	Stakeholder map
Interview 8–12 people across functions	Governance pain points and value themes
Develop and socialise the governance vision	Vision statement and 1-page summary
Pick a lighthouse use case (e.g., customer, product, supplier data)	Scope for initial implementation
Secure executive sponsorship	Named sponsor(s) and support commitments

End of Month 1 Deliverable:

Governance vision, Use case scope, and buy-in from stakeholders

Phase 2: Days 31–60 — Design and Pilot

Goal: Define your framework, assign roles, and launch your first pilot.

Task	Output
Define governance roles (Owner, Steward, Custodian)	RACI matrix and named roles
Draft and approve 3–5 key policies (ownership, quality, access)	Policy documents
Develop glossary and standards for pilot domain	Data definitions, formats, and business terms
Choose governance tooling (catalogue, DQ monitoring, MDM if needed)	Tool shortlist or proof-of-concept
Train pilot stewards and stakeholders	Role-based enablement content
Stand up first issue logging and data quality dashboard	Issue tracker and scorecard prototype

End of Month 2 Deliverable:

Live pilot of governance policies, Stewardship, and Data monitoring in one domain

Phase 3: Days 61–100 — Prove Value and Scale

Goal: Track success, refine approach, and prepare to scale across domains.

Task	Output
Review pilot outcomes and gather feedback	Lessons learned summary
Refine policies, glossary, and processes based on usage	Updated documentation and standards
Create a governance dashboard with business-aligned KPIs	Visual dashboard (e.g., Power BI, Tableau)
Present results to governance council and exec sponsors	Success metrics and scaling proposal
Onboard second domain for governance (e.g., finance or HR)	Extended implementation plan

Launch internal comms campaign (newsletter, spotlight stories)	Engagement and awareness materials

End of Month 3 Deliverable:

Validated pilot, Scaling plan, and Organisation-wide visibility

FINAL THOUGHTS

Data governance is not about control — it is about clarity, confidence, and capability. Whether you are solving for compliance, enabling analytics, or preparing for AI, governance is the key that unlocks the value of your data.

Start small. Anchor your efforts in real business needs. Celebrate wins, learn from friction, and grow your programme one domain, one process, and one steward at a time.

The future belongs to organisations that trust their data - and know how to govern it.

APPENDICES

A. Sample Governance Charter Template

B. Example Data Quality Scorecard

C. RACI Matrix Examples

D. Metadata Glossary Sample

E. Policy Templates (Ownership, Access, Quality)

F. Steward Onboarding Checklist

G. Tool Evaluation Criteria

APPENDICES

Appendix A: Sample Data Governance Charter Template

Purpose:

To establish a formal structure for data governance within the organisation.

Key Components

- Governance Vision and Mission
- Scope (e.g., domains covered)
- Governance Roles (Council, Stewards, Owners)
- Operating Model (centralized, federated, hybrid)
- Decision-Making and Escalation Processes
- Success Metrics and Reporting

Appendix B: Example Data Quality Scorecard

Data Domain	CDE	Accuracy (%)	Completeness (%)	Timeliness	Owner
Customer	Email Address	96%	98%	Daily	Jane Doe
Product	SKU	99%	100%	Real-time	John Smith

Include colour-coded thresholds: Green (95%+), Amber (90-95%), Red (<90%).

Appendix C: RACI Matrix Examples

Activity	Data Owner	Data Steward	IT	Compliance
Define Business Terms	A	R	C	I
Approve Data Quality Rules	A	R	C	C
Implement Metadata Standards	C	R	A	I

A = Accountable,   **R** = Responsible,   **C** = Consulted,   **I** = Informed

Appendix D: Metadata Glossary Sample

Term	Definition	Owner	Last Reviewed
Customer ID	Unique identifier assigned to a customer	CRM Manager	Jan 2025
Invoice Date	Date when invoice is issued to customer	Finance	Feb 2025

Appendix E: Policy Templates

Ownership Policy

- All data domains must have an assigned Data Owner and Steward.
- Owners are accountable for quality, access, and business relevance.

Access Policy

- Access is role-based and reviewed quarterly.
- Sensitive data access must be approved by both Owner and Compliance.

Data Quality Policy

- Quality rules must be defined for all critical data elements.
- Threshold breaches trigger automated alerts to stewards and owner

Appendix F: Steward Onboarding Checklist

- ✓ Welcome and Role Overview
- ✓ Training on Governance Framework

✓ Access to Data Catalogue and Issue Tracker
✓ Introduction to Assigned Domain
✓ Define First 3 Quality Rules
✓ Join Steward Community Channel
✓ Monthly Check-In Scheduled

Appendix G: Tool Evaluation Criteria

Criteria	Description	Priority (1-5)
Usability	Intuitive UI for business and IT users	5
Integration	Connects to existing data sources/tools	5
Lineage Capability	Visual traceability of data flow	4
Quality Monitoring	Rule configuration and alerts	5
Metadata Management	Glossary, tagging, stewardship support	5
Cost and Licensing	Transparent, scalable pricing	4
Vendor Support	Documentation, training, customer service	4

SYNOPSIS

GROUNDED GOVERNANCE: A PRACTICAL GUIDE TO IMPLEMENTING DATA GOVERNANCE THAT WORKS

by Dr. Adetokunbo Ajibola

In today's data-driven world, organisations are flooded with information — but starved of clarity, consistency, and trust. Grounded Governance is the essential guide for business and technology leaders who are ready to turn data chaos into confidence, compliance, and competitive advantage.

Drawing on over 25 years of global experience across finance, telecoms, pharmaceuticals, utilities, and government — including executive roles in the Middle East — Dr. Adetokunbo Ajibola, widely known as *The Data Evangelist*, distils a career's worth of insight into a clear, practical roadmap for implementing data governance that actually works.

From building the business case to assigning roles, launching stewardship, writing enforceable policies, and scaling with the right tools — this book bridges strategy and execution. It speaks to real-world practitioners, not theorists, and delivers sector-specific examples, downloadable templates, and a 100-day starter plan that organisations can use immediately.

Whether you are a Chief Data Officer, data steward, IT leader, or transformation executive, *Grounded Governance* will equip you to:

- Launch a sustainable governance programme that earns business buy-in
- Improve data quality, compliance, and reporting accuracy
- Govern master, reference, and metadata in practical terms
- Prepare your organisation for AI governance and ethical risk
- Drive cultural change through training, communication, and accountability

If you have ever been told *"We don't have time for data governance,"* this book will show you — step by step — why you can't afford not to.

———◆❰❱◆———

Glossary — With Chapter References

How to use: Definitions are concise and mapped to chapters from the reference text "Grounded Governance: A Practical Guide to Implementing Data Governance That Works". References appear as [Ref: Ch.X].

Mini Index (A–Z)

A, B, C, D, E, F, G, K, M, P, R, S, T, U, V

A

Access & Security Policy: Rules that govern role-based access, approvals, authentication and data classification to ensure only authorised users can see or change data. [Ref: Ch.6; Ch.10]

AI Governance: Applying governance to AI/ML models: ownership, lineage, training-data quality, bias/fairness tests, model monitoring and regulatory compliance. [Ref: Ch.14]

B

Business Case (for DG): A narrative linking data governance to risk reduction, revenue enablement and efficiency, with an ROI and cost-of-inaction view. [Ref: Ch.3]

Business Glossary: Authoritative business definitions and allowable values for terms used across the organisation, owned by stewards and surfaced in the data catalogue. [Ref: Ch.8]

C

Change Request (Data): A controlled workflow to propose, assess, approve and implement changes to definitions, rules, standards or metadata. [Ref: Ch.4; Ch.6]

Collibra — Key Terms: Communities, Domains, Assets, Steward/Owner roles, Workflows, Policies; typically surfaced through the data catalogue. [Ref: Ch.10]

Critical Data Elements (CDEs): High-impact data fields essential to operations, reporting or analytics; prioritised for quality rules, ownership and controls. [Ref: Ch.7]

D

Data Catalogue: A searchable inventory of data assets showing definitions, ownership, lineage, classifications and usage context. [Ref: Ch.8]

Data Custodian: Technology role accountable for secure storage, backup, technical controls and performance of data platforms in line with policy. [Ref: Ch.5]

Data Domain: A logical business area grouping related data (e.g., Customer, Product, Finance) with defined owners and stewards. [Ref: Ch.4; Ch.5]

Data Governance (DG): Decision rights, policies, standards and processes that ensure data is accurate, secure, accessible and usable enterprise-wide. [Ref: Ch.1]

Data Governance Charter: Concise document defining purpose, scope, roles, operating model and success metrics for governance. [Ref: Appendix A]

Data Governance Council: Cross-functional leadership forum that sets priorities, approves policy/standards and resolves escalations. [Ref: Ch.5]

Data Governance Framework: The operating model covering principles, roles, policies, processes, tooling and metrics for governing data. [Ref: Ch.4]

Data Governance Maturity Assessment: Baseline assessment of ownership, quality, metadata, lineage, tooling and culture to prioritise quick wins and roadmap. [Ref: Ch.2]

Data Lineage: End-to-end traceability of data flow from source to consumption, including transformations, for audit and impact analysis. [Ref: Ch.8; Ch.10]

Data Owner: Senior business role accountable for data within a domain, including quality, access decisions and acceptable use. [Ref: Ch.5]

Data Privacy: Practices and controls ensuring lawful, fair and transparent processing of personal data (e.g., GDPR, NDPR). [Ref: Ch.10]

Data Product: A high-quality, well-defined data set or service designed for reuse, with SLAs, documentation, ownership and quality measures. [Ref: Ch.2; Ch.4]

Data Quality (DQ): Fitness of data for its intended use; managed via rules, monitoring, remediation and continuous improvement. [Ref: Ch.7]

Data Quality Dimensions: Common dimensions include Accuracy, Completeness, Consistency, Timeliness, Validity and Uniqueness. [Ref: Ch.7]

Data Quality Issue Management: Log → classify → assign → remediate → verify → close, with root-cause analysis and audit trail. [Ref: Ch.7]

Data Standards: Agreed formats, naming conventions and validation rules that drive consistency and interoperability. [Ref: Ch.6]

Data Steward: Subject-matter expert responsible for definitions, rules, metadata and day-to-day quality within a domain. [Ref: Ch.5]

E

Exception Review: Formal process to approve temporary deviations from a policy or standard with compensating controls. [Ref: Ch.4; Ch.6]

F

Framework Models (Operating): Centralised, Federated and Hybrid ways of organising governance roles and decision rights across the enterprise. [Ref: Ch.4]

G

Golden Record: The authoritative, deduplicated master view of an entity (e.g., customer) used consistently across systems. [Ref: Ch.9]

K

KPI Tiers (for DG): Strategic, operational and data-quality KPIs that evidence governance outcomes on dashboards. [Ref: Ch.12]

M

Master Data: Core, non-transactional entities shared across processes (Customer, Product, Supplier, Account, Location). [Ref: Ch.9]

Master Data Management (MDM) Models: Registry, Consolidation, Coexistence and Centralised patterns used to master and distribute golden records. [Ref: Ch.9]

Metadata: 'Data about data' providing business, technical and operational context to interpret and trust data. [Ref: Ch.8]

Microsoft Purview — Key Terms: Collections, Glossary Terms, Scans, Classifications, Sensitivity Labels, Data Lineage and Access policies. [Ref: Ch.10]

P

PDCA Cycle: Plan-Do-Check-Act loop used to drive continuous improvement of governance processes and outcomes. [Ref: Ch.12]

Policy / Standard / Procedure: Policy = what must be done; Standard = how data should conform; Procedure = step-by-step actions. [Ref: Ch.6]

R

RACI: Matrix clarifying responsibility: Responsible, Accountable, Consulted, Informed for each activity. [Ref: Appendix C]

Reference Data: Controlled code lists and allowable values (e.g., country codes, currency, risk ratings) used across systems. [Ref: Ch.9]

Reltio — Key Terms: Entities & Relationships, Match/Merge, Survivorship, Cross-walks, Reference Data, L2 attributes and APIs. [Ref: Ch.9; Ch.10]

S

Stewardship Forum: Recurring session where owners and stewards review quality, issues, risks and improvement actions. [Ref: Ch.4]

T

Tooling Categories: Catalogue/metadata, data-quality, MDM/RDM, policy/workflow, access/security and integration/automation platforms. [Ref: Ch.10]

U

Use-Case 'Lighthouse': A narrow, high-value scope that proves governance value quickly before scaling to other domains. [Ref: Ch.2]

V

Vision & Scope (DG): Statement linking governance aims to business strategy and a bounded first domain with measurable outcomes. [Ref: Ch.2–3]

Abbreviations

AI: Artificial Intelligence

BCBS 239: Basel Committee principles for effective risk data aggregation and reporting

CDMP: Certified Data Management Professional

CDE: Critical Data Element

DAMA-DMBOK: Data Management Body of Knowledge by DAMA International

DG: Data Governance

DQ: Data Quality

ETL/ELT: Extract-Transform-Load / Extract-Load-Transform

GDPR: General Data Protection Regulation (EU/UK)

KPI: Key Performance Indicator

MDM: Master Data Management

NDPR: Nigeria Data Protection Regulation

PII: Personally Identifiable Information

RACI: Responsible, Accountable, Consulted, Informed

SLA: Service Level Agreement

www.ingramcontent.com/pod-product-compliance
Lightning Source LLC
Chambersburg PA
CBHW071504210326
41597CB00018B/2680